BIG JIM

Jim Larkin and the 1913 Lockout

Rory McConville & Paddy Lynch

THE O'BRIEN PRESS
DUBLIN

Dedication

To Miriam and Eugene McConville for all their encouragement and support.

Acknowledgements

I would like to thank Padraig Yeates for his assistance and for his book *Lockout 1913*, which was an invaluable resource. Thanks also to the University College Cork Multitext Project. Thanks to Michael, Ivan, Emma, Mary and all the staff at The O'Brien Press for all the hard work they've put into this book. Thanks to Paddy Lynch for being a great collaborator.

Thanks to my family for putting up with me. R McC

Dedication

To Katie Blackwood, for enduring the late nights and for the constant support and encouragement.

Acknowledgements

I would like to acknowledge and thank Rory for being such an open collaborator, Emma Byrne, Mary Webb and everyone at The O'Brien Press for advice, patience and faith in the project, Padraig Yeates for the historical fact checking, Phil Barrett for being such an excellent sounding board, and Declan Shalvey for the recommendation at the very beginning. PL

RORY McCONVILLE is a writer from Cork. He has worked as a graphic novelist for several years, writing for companies such as DC Comics.

PADDY LYNCH is a cartoonist and designer from Dublin. This is his first full length graphic novel, his other comics and illustrations can be viewed at www.patrickl.net.

25 August 1913. Temple Lane, off Parnell Street in the tenements of inner city Dublin...

wwWWAAGH!

wwWWAAGH!

wwWWAAGH!

What are we going to do, Tom? What?! We've no food, no money...

Kitty, can't you shut him up for one second?!?

I... I have to pee...

Dublin docks.

26 August 1913.

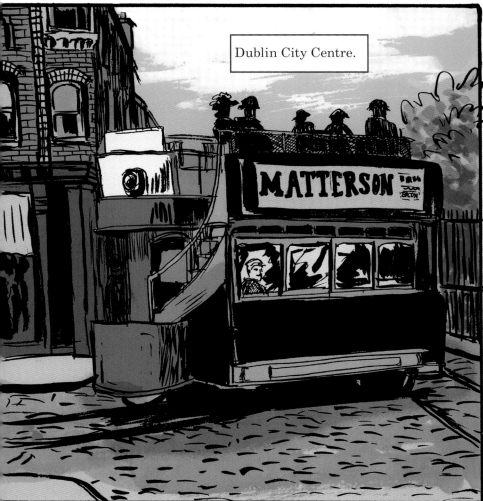

Dublin City Centre.

MATTERSON

Here...

wha?

Lookit.

Oh, right –

The horse show's on today.

Paddy.

Are you coming?

I've got a wife and three kids.

Well, I hope they're *proud* of their *SCAB!*

Later that evening.

'The trams were back moving within, I'd say, forty minutes. An hour maybe.'

What would you say?

I'd say about forty minutes.

I'd say only about half of them went on strike.

It was 200, actually. Out of 650.

NUDGE!

See? Not much of a strike at all really.

Liberty Hall.

Headquarters of the Irish Transport & General Workers Union.

'It is not a strike, but a lockout of men, who have been tyrannically treated by a most unscrupulous scoundrel.'

'Murphy has boasted that he will beat Larkin. What a wonderful boast.'

'He said he would spend £100,000 to break Larkin, a man who is going to lead you out of bondage into the land of promise.'

'The cars are taken off the street at seven o'clock. Murphy is a coward. If I had the same power behind me as Murphy, I would take the cars out night, noon and morning.'

'Murphy talked of Larkin biting a file but if it were not for Larkin the trams would be running until 12 o'clock tonight.'

And so –
I WON THE FIRST ROUND!

28 August, Dublin Castle. Magistrate Swifte's hearing.

And is it true that you have announced a meeting to be held in Sackville Street at the weekend?

Yes, your honour.

You are released on bail under the condition that you will not hold any meetings or invoke seditious language.

Thank you, your honour.

Ah here...

What's the matter with you?

The government's gone and banned the bloody meeting on Sunday!

Well, what did you expect? Sure aren't they all in cahoots with each other?

Surrey House, Rathmines.

Home of Count and Countess Markievicz.

I told you, Constance, I *don't* want him here!

And I don't really care, my dear. He's my guest, and he *stays*.

You *know* the police are watching. We need to—

Well, we'll just have to distract them. I've been meaning to throw a party anyway.

That night.

I guess he mustn't be here.

Larkin wasn't at the house, sir.

Forget about that. You're going straight back out there.

There's been rioting for the whole day.

30 August.

SCABS

Shelbourne Football Club, Ringsend.

It's all Larkin's fault. He told them there were scabs on the Bohs team.

Come on and get killed!

SCABS!

They all started crowding outside the stadium, shouting and screaming.

I mean, what did he think was going to happen?

We were dealing with those animals until three in the morning.

Lads, I'm done in.

Once you get a jar into you, you'll be alright.

Are you right there, Smith?

...and then back out for this?

I'm just so tired.

of all the...

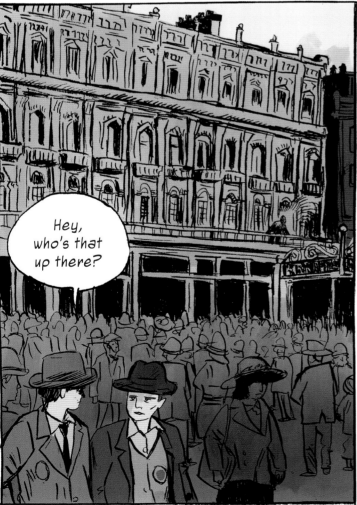

Come on, ye bowsies, we dare ye!

We just came to see the Horse Show. First last night, and now this.

You people are nothing short of animals!

I could smell stout on their breath. They were all dr—

unnhuh

31 August 1913.

Bloody Sunday.

Until further notice, Jacobs will not be requiring your services.

You can all work on the condition that you remove your union badges.

We will not be reopening until we're certain that we have a sufficiently loyal labour force.

Our problem isn't with trade unionism, it's with Larkin. This isn't about us, this is about one man, James Larkin, trying to rule the trade of Dublin. So until that changes, we're closed for the foreseeable future.

I told you explicitly not to hold or attend the meeting.

And then you went ahead and held the meeting.

Magistrate Swifte's courtroom.

It hardly needs to be said - bail is *refused*.

29

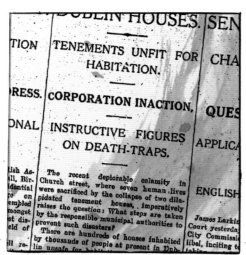

DUBLIN HOUSES. SEN

TENEMENTS UNFIT FOR HABITATION.

CORPORATION INACTION,

INSTRUCTIVE FIGURES ON DEATH-TRAPS.

The recent deplorable calamity in Church street, where seven human lives were sacrificed by the collapse of two dilapidated tenement houses, imperatively raises the question: What steps are taken by the responsible municipal authorities to prevent such disasters?

There are hundreds of houses inhabited by thousands of people at present in Dublin unsafe for habitation.

It's lucky only seven poor souls died that night - and these are the kind of conditions we have to live in, is it?

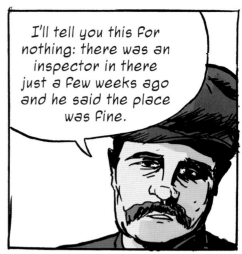

I'll tell you this for nothing: there was an inspector in there just a few weeks ago and he said the place was fine.

The British Trades Union Congress.

Milton Hall, Manchester.

This is a disaster!

All of our members want to strike with the Irish.

But why do we have to help them? We just finished our own strike.

If we do nothing, the members are certain to be done with us.

LIBERTY HA

'The British Trades Union Congress want us to send over a delegation...'

William Partridge

They're going to strike in with us. I know it.

I just know it!

It's certainly encouraging

Larkin is a menace. And something needs to be done about him.

William Martin Murphy addresses a meeting of Dublin employers.

I propose that we unite and form an Employers' Federation.

I also propose the creation of a document that will ensure the loyalty of our workers.

And so...

I hereby undertake to carry out all instructions given to me by or on behalf of my employers, and further, I agree to immediately resign my membership of the ITGWU (if a member) and I further undertake that I will not join or in any way support this union.

Signed

I refuse.

You've got a wife and six children. They'll starve because of this.

I'd rather see them in coffins than disgrace them by signing this.

3 September.

Inquest into the death of James Nolan.

It's been confirmed by multiple witnesses that the deceased was left lying unattended on the quayside for over twenty minutes.

Yes.

It's been established that the fatal blow came from a police baton.

However, we can't really determine who struck the blow.

HERE LIES OUR BRO

JAMES NOL

Speaking on behalf of the British Trades Unions, we are outraged. What is being done to you workers is outrageous and should be stopped at all costs.

Keir Hardie.

Hey! HEY! On behalf of every starving, jobless soul here - are you going to help us stop it?

Well ... we haven't really made up our minds yet.

What about us?! There's 15,000 of us locked out!

That's pretty weak.

15,000, is that an accurate figure?

Yes.

...oh...

Larkin speaks in Manchester.

We need the help of you, our fellow workers. We would ask that you help us in our cause.

Meanwhile, in Liverpool.

We're not touching those boxes.

They're heading to Jacobs factory in Dublin. They're tainted goods.

Why?

The Irish workers need help, they need donations.

Encourage your trade union leaders to dig deep into their pockets and help us.

We are offering £5,000 in foodstuffs that will be sent over in a ship in the next few days.

We will also try and raise money from the other unions.

...and finally, I would ask that you appeal to your union leaders to strike in solidarity with us. Together we can create a strike that will stretch the length and breadth of Great Britain!

We will not, however, be engaging in any action beyond this.

Dublin Docklands.

27 September.

It's ridiculous really.

Wouldn't it have made more sense just to send money over so we could buy the food here?

And isn't it a disgrace that we're getting help—

Mammy...

From the *Brits*, of all people.

Mammy!

What?

When's the food getting here?

Go ask your da.

LOOK!

It's The Hare!
They sent it!

I would like to announce that Sir George Askwith has been called in to settle the dispute.

Augustine Birrell, Chief Secretary for Ireland.

The Askwith Inquiry

Dublin Federation of Employers vs the ITGWU

Dublin Castle

Day 1

Do you want to know what Mr Larkin wants?

It's not to help the workers improve their lot in life. It's not to right some sort of social injustice.

T M Healy, Counsel for the Federation of Employers.

He wants simply and totally to be the dictator of all the trade in Dublin.

We had an agreement with the ITGWU that was signed only four days ago.

We would withhold tainted goods and would, as such, be allowed to go about our business.

But so far, no workers have arrived!

It's no wonder the Employers' Federation will not speak with them. Their word is worth absolutely nothing.

The Askwith Inquiry, Day 2.

William Martin Murphy is called on to speak.

Have they started yet?

I don't think Larkin's arrived.

'Is this the first time they've met face to face?'

I am not opposed to trade unionism.

My problem is purely with *Larkin* and the ITGWU.

Then *why* have you been involved in crushing so many strikes?

Would you tell us what you call intimidation?

Is it intimidation to say to a man, 'Will you belong to this union or that union?'

That is *not* intimidation.

'If you join a certain union you will be deprived of your livelihood and your children will starve.'

-is that intimidation?

I don't think so.

42

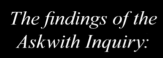

The findings of the Askwith Inquiry:

'The sympathetic strike is a dangerous tool and by using it, damages all potential industrial relations.'

'However, similarly the use of a written agreement that employees must sign is deplorable and imposes on its signatories conditions that are contrary to individual liberty.'

'Therefore, we propose the formation of a conciliation board.'

Joe! What's the good word? Are we going back to work?

The employers rejected it. What did you expect?

Don't know why I'm surprised.

Has Larkin said anything?

He's headed back to England to protest.

Manchester.

I SAY *TO HELL* WITH THE CONTRACTS!

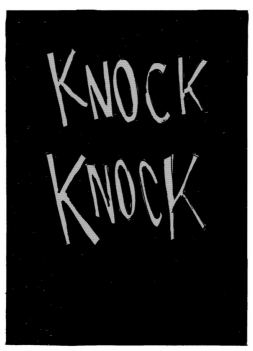

KNOCK KNOCK

Yes? Can I help you?

Delia Larkin.

Liberty Hall.

Hello Delia. My name is Dora Montefiore, I talked with your brother in Manchester.

We're here to help save the Irish kiddies.

Our plan is to give your children happy homes in England until this conflict is over.

We will only be taking children whose...

whose parents are involved in the strike" was the explanation given by Ms. Montefiore yesterday.

FEARED TROUBLE IN WATERFOR
Anoth ...reatened at Wat
Clyde Sh
igume

Archbishop Walsh.

This will not do.

46

All of the families have been properly vetted and we can promise that they will be well looked after while in our care.

Have the parents of Ireland abandoned their faith? I sincerely hope not. Mothers who partake in this will no longer be worthy of the name of Catholic mothers.

Do you know if these childminders are Catholic?

Are they even religious at *all*?

You have my word that these parents are perfectly acceptable and-

Her word? What use is her word to us?

This cannot be allowed to pass. It is an outrage.

We're just trying to help.

I do not expect that decent Catholics will allow this to happen.

We do not want English charity.

Our first departure will be tomorrow.

The next day.

Don't take away our children.

I don't care what they say. I want my children out of this wretched place.

Almost there now, children!

Mrs Montefiore, The priests are here.

Give us the children!

MY FRIENDS!

Please! Be *calm!*

Look!

The children are here. They're quite safe!

He's a great man, no doubt about that...

...but if he comes between me and my religion, he'd better watch himself.

I'll tell you what we're doing: we're making sure no one tries to send our children away. We won't let them corrupt our young.

We kept trying for the next couple of days. In the end, we only got two groups of sixteen children.

At least that's something.

I swear to you, James, these priests, these so-called 'holy men' are a disgrace to their cloth. It's enough to make you sick.

What good is any religion that can't stand a fortnight's holiday in England?

Even still, Jim, we've lost a lot of support because of this scheme.

The way they're behaving, I'd be willing to bet half of the clergy must have shares in the tram companies!!

Did I know? No, of course not. They told me that they were sending my child to a school up the country. If I'd known, I would have never let them do it.

None of the children have attended mass. It's an absolute disgrace. And you know—

Excuse me, Father Fleming?

Could you possibly move a little bit to your left?

Oh, sorry. Is here better?

Perfect.

TUC offices, London.

We need to state that we had no involvement in trying to transport children here.

And we need to take a slight step back from Larkin. He's really started making a mess of this.

It was an idiotic move on Larkin's part. He'll have everyone turning against him.

So, we're agreed. We'll continue to send provisions as well as money... anything else?

Yes, they'll have to open negotiations with the employers.

Liberty Hall.

James Larkin, this court finds you guilty of sedition!

27 October.

You are hereby sentenced to **seven months' hard labour,** to begin immediately.

That should be it, then.

Yes, we'll just let it die slowly now.

Liberty Hall.

We have to do something! We need to get Larkin out.

Aren't there a couple of important by-elections coming up in England?

55

What if we sent men over to campaign against the government's candidates?

I believe so. But what use are they to us?

No support unless Larkin is freed! They won't be able to ignore us then.

First by-election, Reading.

I will provide strong leadership.

The government's candidate, George Peabody Gooch

FREE LARKIN!

Excuse me?

FREE LARKIN!

Later.

The results of the Reading by-election of 1913 are as follows...

Wilson, Unionist Candidate, 5144 Votes
Gooch, Liberal Candidate, 4013 Votes
Butler, Socialist Candidate, 1063 Votes

Westminster.

We've lost Reading and barely held onto Linlithgow.

Because of Larkin?

I can't deny it was a factor.

Well, you'll just have to release him, then, won't you?

The government made a mistake in sending me to jail but they made an even bigger one by releasing me. This fight is only starting!

I will be leaving shortly, leaving for Britain where I will rouse the workers of England, Scotland and Wales...

With their help, we are going to create a strike that stretches across the *whole* United Kingdom.

Is that a food ship?

I thought we weren't getting one for another couple of days.

No. By God, no.

I'll tell you what that is...

That's a scab labour ship!

Out on the streets all over the city.

SCABS!

GERROUTOVIT YOU BLOODY SCABS!

GO HOME!

The work needs to be done, and if they're not going to do it, I will. I've got a wife and kids too, y'know. And I need to look after them.

Someone told me that the scabs are allowed to carry guns. Is that true?

Well of course we do. They'd murder us otherwise. I was walking home the other day and some blokes just started chucking stuff at us.

On the docks.

You docker lads are coming out on strike with us. From today.

What? But why?

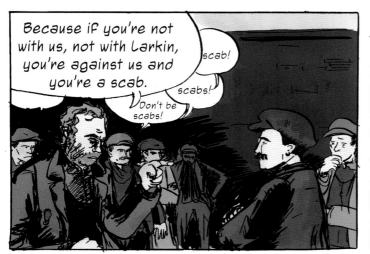

Because if you're not with us, not with Larkin, you're against us and you're a scab.

scab!

scabs!

Don't be scabs!

sigh

Okay, lads, down tools. We're on strike.

what?!

why?

s'not our fault they're on strike!

If you have a problem, discuss it with these gentlemen from Larkin's union.

We're on strike.

Workers' marches come under continual harassment from the Dublin Metropolitan Police.

Bloody Larkinites! Get out of here!

Get out of the way. The trams are coming.

Captain White will speak to you now and tell you of his plans to create a great Citizen Army from among the members of the labour unions.

I want all men to appear at Croydon Park, Fairview tomorrow, where our training will begin.

'We will pass out your weapons and show you how to put manners on the Dublin Metropolitan Police!'

Are you the captain of this march?

Yes.

Could you allow the trams to pass?

Of course. All you had to do was ask.

Stand down! Let the trams through.

At a Trade Union rally in Manchester.

Strike in solidarity with us.

I'm not going to stop. I'm not going to give up until the workers are given their due!

And I want you to help...

'We will win this!'

He must be exhausted.

He's doing two to three meetings a night...

No man can keep that type of intensity up indefinitely.

Well, we'll see what the Union leaders say tomorrow.

64

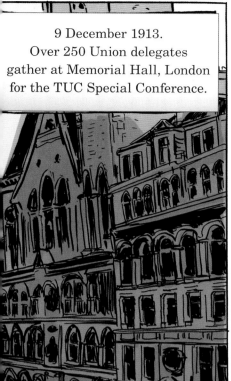

9 December 1913.
Over 250 Union delegates gather at Memorial Hall, London for the TUC Special Conference.

Ahem.

Mr Chairman and human beings...

It was horrible, really, there was just shouting and shouting. Larkin couldn't even say a word without being booed.

Who does he think he is to come in here and condemn us? All we've done is help, and not one word of thanks.

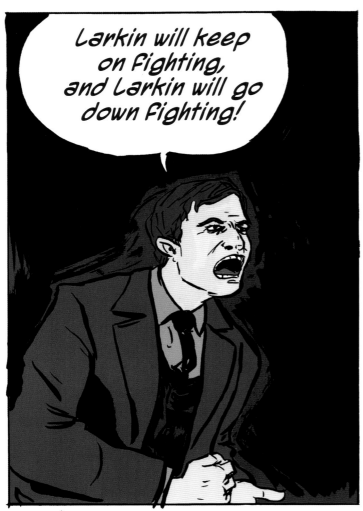

On the return journey.

Talks between the ITGWU and the Employers' Federation recommence.

It's come to our attention that a number of changes have been made to the agenda. Specifically, the reinstatement of workers.

As has been explained already, we are not in a position to re-employ all workers. We'd appreciate if we could come to some sort of compromise.

No.

No?

Our demands have been clearly stated.

We will not be accepting *anything* less.

I repeat:
All the workers will be reinstated.

70

RESULTS OF THE DUBLIN HOUSING INQUIRY

We have observed that in 8,914 of the 21,113 single roomed tenements, there is no overcrowding.

I have been working in the north inner city. I have seen houses where 107 people share two outhouses.

There is no city that I know which requires a more extensive system of housing improvement than Dublin.

FINDINGS OF THE DUBLIN DISTURBANCES COMMISSION.

The officers and men of the Dublin Metropolitan Police and the Royal Irish Constabulary, as a whole, discharged their duties throughout this trying period with conspicuous courage and patience.

So those *OMP thugs* get off scot free as usual? Nothing strange there...

Dublin, June 1914.

It took a while, but eventually people started drifting back. They realised that the employers weren't going to fire them.

The employers wouldn't be stupid enough to try another lockout. Losing £200,000 a month? Not a chance.

14 October 1914.

It'll be nice to rest for a while.

Well, you've surely earned it.

Do you think it made a difference?

I have no doubt!

Do you think the workers of Dublin will ever allow themselves to be so mistreated again?

I'm glad that it did some good!

The Lockout had changed things in Dublin, and indeed Ireland, forever.

Following 1913, no employer ever again attempted to break workers in the same manner as William Martin Murphy.

James Connolly continued to lead the Irish Citizens Army and fought in the 1916 Easter Rising.

Wounded in action in the GPO, he was captured and executed in Kilmainham Gaol.

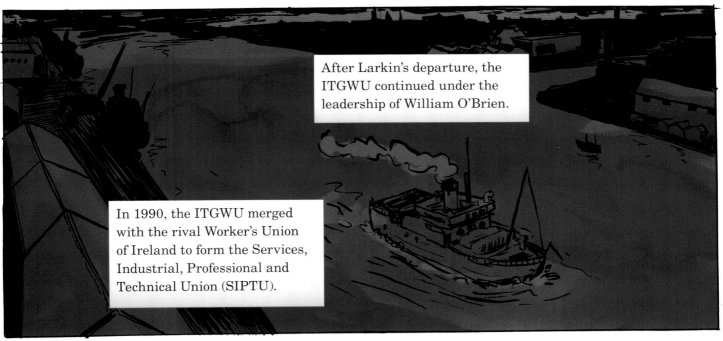

After Larkin's departure, the ITGWU continued under the leadership of William O'Brien.

In 1990, the ITGWU merged with the rival Worker's Union of Ireland to form the Services, Industrial, Professional and Technical Union (SIPTU).

James Larkin travelled to America in 1914 to recover from the physical and mental exhaustion of the Lockout.

While there, he fundraised for the ITGWU and became involved in the Socialist Party of America and the Industrial Workers of the World.

He returned to Ireland in 1923, receiving a hero's welcome.

The Labour Leader would continue to fight for workers' rights until his death in 1947.